contents

Key

Number and Place Value

Addition and Subtraction

Multiplication and Division

Shape and Measure

Fractions and Decimals

Mixed Operations

How to use this book

This book is a little different from your workbook! Follow the instructions and write the questions and answers out in your own maths book.

The first page of each section will have a title telling you what the next few pages are about.

Read the instructions carefully before each set of questions.

Some pages will show you an example or model.

Your teacher may tell you to GRAB something that might help you answer the questions.

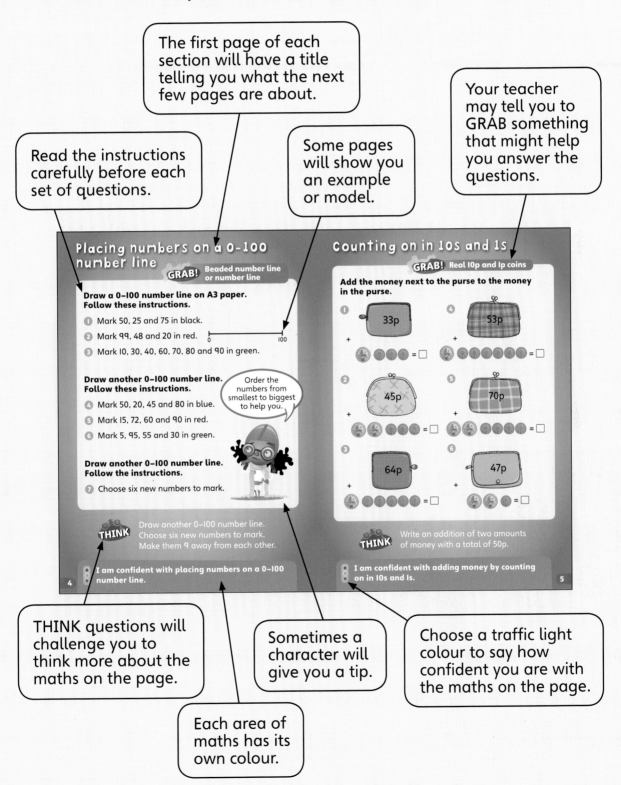

THINK questions will challenge you to think more about the maths on the page.

Each area of maths has its own colour.

Sometimes a character will give you a tip.

Choose a traffic light colour to say how confident you are with the maths on the page.

Placing numbers on a 0–100 number line

GRAB! Beaded number line or number line

Draw a 0–100 number line on A3 paper. Follow these instructions.

1. Mark 50, 25 and 75 in black.

2. Mark 99, 48 and 20 in red.

|———————————————|
0   100

3. Mark 10, 30, 40, 60, 70, 80 and 90 in green.

Draw another 0–100 number line. Follow these instructions.

4. Mark 50, 20, 45 and 80 in blue.

5. Mark 15, 72, 60 and 90 in red.

6. Mark 5, 95, 55 and 30 in green.

> Order the numbers from smallest to biggest to help you.

Draw another 0–100 number line. Follow the instructions.

7. Choose six new numbers to mark.

 **THINK** Draw another 0–100 number line. Choose six new numbers to mark. Make them 9 away from each other.

○
○ **I am confident with placing numbers on a 0–100**
○ **number line.**

Counting on in 10s and 1s

Add the money next to the purse to the money in the purse.

1  33p

+  = ☐

4  53p

+ = ☐

2  45p

+  = ☐

5  70p

+  = ☐

3  64p

+  = ☐

6 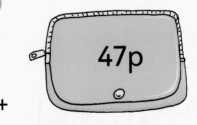 47p

+  = ☐

 **THINK** Write an addition of two amounts of money with a total of 50p.

○
○ **I am confident with adding money by counting**
○ **on in 10s and 1s.**

5

Complete these additions.

① 53 + 42 = ☐

⑤ 85 + 41 = ☐

② 63 + 26 = ☐

⑥ 96 + 22 = ☐

③ 35 + 44 = ☐

⑦ 33 + 92 = ☐

④ 24 + 71 = ☐

Work out the missing number.

⑧ 43 + ☐ = 68

⑨ 89 + ☐ = 100

Remember to put the bigger number first.

THINK

Write an addition of three amounts of money that has a total of 50p.

I am confident with counting on in 10s and 1s.

6

Bonds to 10 and doubles

Complete these additions.

1. 6 + 8 + 6 = ☐

2. 3 + 8 + 7 = ☐

3. 5 + 9 + 5 = ☐

4. 4 + 7 + 6 = ☐

5. 9 + 8 + 2 = ☐

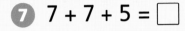

6. 4 + 8 + 4 = ☐

7. 7 + 7 + 5 = ☐

8. 8 + 4 + 6 = ☐

9. 9 + 9 + 6 = ☐

10. 7 + 9 + 7 = ☐

THINK

**Can you score 16 points?
Play Magic 16 using these rules.**

How many sets of three numbers can you write that have a total of 16? Score 1 point for each set. Score an extra point for any set that contains a double. Score an extra point for any set that contains a bond to 10.

○
○ **I am confident with adding bonds to 10 and**
○ **doubles.**

Answer these questions using doubling.

What numbers will come out of the machine if these go in?

① 13   ③ 21   ⑤ 12   ⑦ 24

② 14   ④ 31   ⑥ 41   ⑧ 25

These numbers came out of the machine. What numbers went in?

⑨ 30   ⑪ 64

⑩ 86   ⑫ 42

THINK   The machine is broken.
23 was put in and 47 came out.
What is wrong with the machine?

I am confident with doubling 2-digit numbers.

Subtracting by counting back in 10s and 1s

Choose a planet number and subtract a star number. Write the answer.
Do this ten times.

1	2	3	4	5	6	7	8	9	10
11	12	13	14	15	16	17	18	19	20
21	22	23	24	25	26	27	28	29	30
31	32	33	34	35	36	37	38	39	40
41	42	43	44	45	46	47	48	49	50
51	52	53	54	55	56	57	58	59	60
61	62	63	64	65	66	67	68	69	70
71	72	73	74	75	76	77	78	79	80
81	82	83	84	85	86	87	88	89	90
91	92	93	94	95	96	97	98	99	100

THINK Choose three of your answers. Check them by using addition.

○
○ I am confident with subtracting by counting
○ back in 10s and 1s.

Complete these subtractions by counting back in 10s and using number facts.

GRAB! 100-square

59 − 36 = 23

1 37 − 24 = ☐

2 65 − 13 = ☐

3 46 − 32 = ☐

4 79 − 17 = ☐

5 26 − 23 = ☐

6 88 − 44 = ☐

7 37 − 13 = ☐

8 54 − 22 = ☐

9 98 − 56 = ☐

10 69 − 33 = ☐

11 86 − 52 = ☐

12 Choose three of the subtractions.
Write the number fact you had to use.

For example: 59 − 36 = 23 ⟶ 9 − 6 = 3

THINK

☐☐ − ☐☐ = ☐☐

Write three subtractions like this where you would use the number fact 5 − 4 = 1.

I am confident with counting back in 10s and using number facts to subtract.

Adding 2-digit numbers

Add the scores.

GRAB! 100-square

Sian	Jerry
34	25

34 + 25 = 59

6

Aiza	Simon
34	69

1

Tom	Precious
42	27

7

Katia	Theo
17	84

2

Jay	Ellie
53	35

8

Dean	Cho
23	85

3

Nat	Lucy
62	34

9

Rahim	Tahlia
97	31

4

Emma	Mario
45	36

10

Dan	Faith
44	73

5

Rima	Anshu
28	57

11

Nina	Zoya
57	61

THINK Olivia estimates the answer to her sum is 50. One of the numbers she adds is 15. What is the other number?

I am confident with adding 2-digit numbers by counting on.

Remember to start with the bigger number!

16 + 47 = ☐
47 + 16 = 63

5 47 + 32 = ☐

1 35 + 32 = ☐

6 35 + 83 = ☐

2 19 + 57 = ☐

7 16 + 71 = ☐

3 28 + 16 = ☐

8 28 + 57 = ☐

4 64 + 28 = ☐

9 71 + 64 = ☐

THINK Choose any 2-digit numbers to write an addition that totals 100. Write four additions like this. Neither 2-digit number should be a multiple of 10.

1 $34 + 23$
$= 50 + 7 = \square$

6 $48 + 35$
$= \square + \square = \square$

2 $47 + 24$
$= 60 + 11 = \square$

7 $74 + 42$
$= \square + \square = \square$

3 $36 + 48$
$= 70 + 14 = \square$

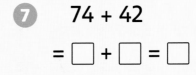

8 $65 + 39$
$= \square + \square = \square$

4 $28 + 16$
$= 30 + 14 = \square$

9 $57 + 47$
$= \square + \square = \square$

5 $64 + 28$
$= 80 + 12 = \square$

10 $63 + 68$
$= \square + \square = \square$

THINK $\quad 4\,\square + 3\,\square = 8\,\square$

What could the missing digits be?

I am confident with adding 2-digit numbers using partitioning.

Measuring capacity

Look at the containers and follow the instructions.

1. Write the letters of the containers that can hold more than a litre of Orange Fizz.

2. Write the letters of the containers that can hold less than a litre of Orange Fizz.

 **THINK** Draw a picture of something in your home that holds more than a litre.

○
○ **I am confident with knowing how much 1 litre is.**
○

Doubling and halving

Double each child's score.

1  15

2  20

3  45

4  30

5  35

6  50

Find half of the money in each purse.

7

8

9

10

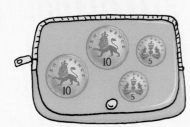 **THINK** Start with 64p. How many times can you split this amount in half?

○
○ I am confident with doubling and halving 2-digit
○ numbers.

Double each amount.

1

4

7

2

5

8

3

6

q

THINK Which coins can you double to get another coin?

I am confident with doubling amounts of money ending in 0, 1 or 2.

Finding $\frac{1}{2}$, $\frac{1}{4}$ and $\frac{1}{3}$

Find $\frac{1}{2}$, $\frac{1}{4}$ and $\frac{1}{3}$ by looking at the olives on the pizzas and the candles on the cakes.

1

$\frac{1}{2}$ of $\boxed{10}$ = $\square$

4

$\frac{1}{4}$ of $\square$ = $\square$

2

$\frac{1}{3}$ of $\square$ = $\square$

5

$\frac{1}{3}$ of $\square$ = $\square$

3

$\frac{1}{2}$ of $\square$ = $\square$

6

$\frac{1}{4}$ of $\square$ = $\square$

 THINK One-quarter of a bag of oranges is 5 oranges. How many oranges are in the whole bag? How many in two bags?

○○○ **I am confident with finding halves, thirds and quarters of a number of objects.**

Subtracting 2-digit numbers

1	2	3	4	5	6	7	8
11	12	13	14	15	16	17	
21	22	23	24	25	26		
31	32	33	34	35			
41	42	43	44				

Complete these subtractions.

1. 57 – 23 = ☐

2. 84 – 52 = ☐

3. 68 – 45 = ☐

4. 95 – 73 = ☐

5. 86 – 45 = ☐

6. 84 – 71 = ☐

Solve these word problems.

7. A teacher opens a new pack of 48 pencils. She gives a pencil to each of the 32 children in her class. How many pencils are now left in the pack?

8. There are 59 elephants. 33 are cooling off in the water. How many are not in the water?

 THINK Make up your own problem for the subtraction 73 – 42.

○ ○ ○ **I am confident with subtracting 2-digit numbers.**

using number facts

Solve these word problems.

1. Mary is playing a game of darts. Her first dart scores 7, her second scores 5 and her third scores 3. What is her total score for the three darts?

2. Claire has three coins. Two are 5p coins and one is a 2p coin. How much money does she have?

3. In a field there are 8 sheep, 3 goats and 8 cows. How many animals are there in total?

4. Zoya has 8 grey pencils, 7 coloured pencils and 2 pens in her pencil case. How many items does she have in her pencil case altogether?

5. Kevin has chicken pox and has 30 spots altogether. He has 7 spots on each arm and 6 spots on his face. How many spots are on the rest of his body?

6. Nicola buys a DVD for £6, a magazine for £4 and a pair of sunglasses for £7. How much change from £20 does she get?

 **THINK** Make up your own problem for the addition 7 + 5 + 7.

O
O   **I am confident with using number facts to solve**
O   **word problems.**

Solve these word problems.

1 In a pot there are 7 green pencils, 8 blue pencils, 6 red pencils and 2 orange ones. How many pencils are there in the pot altogether?

2 On a village pond there are 9 ducks, 5 ducklings, 7 swans and 5 geese. How many birds are there in total?

3 Miss Jones bakes some cakes for the school fair. She bakes 8 fairy cakes, 6 iced buns, 9 fruit scones and 8 doughnuts. If they are all sold for 2p each, how much money is paid in total?

4 Dan is playing a game with four darts. His first dart scores 7, his second scores 5, his third scores 8 and his fourth scores 9. His old score was 25. How many more did he score this time?

5 Amy, Livvy, Sunita and Mohammed agree to put their money together for their school charity appeal. Amy has 5p, Livvy has 7p, Sunita has 9p and Mohammed has 3p. Sunita's mum says she will double their money as it is for a good cause. How much do they give altogether?

6 Chloe and her friends find conkers under a tree. Chloe picks up 9 conkers, Jan picks up 7, Zoe picks up 6 and Rory picks up 8. If there were 40 conkers under the tree, how many did they leave on the ground?

○
○ **I am confident with using number facts to solve**
○ **word problems.**

Recording amounts of money

Write how much money is shown for each question.

1

6

2

7

3

8

4

9

5

10

 **THINK** Choose a total on this page. Think of another way to make that amount.

⊙ **I am confident with adding and recording**
○ **amounts of money.**

Multiplication arrays

Write two multiplication facts for each picture.

1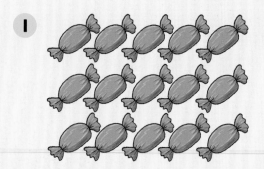

4

2

5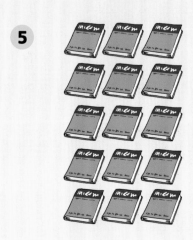

3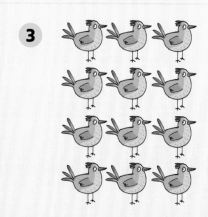

6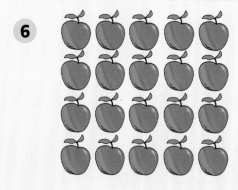

THINK Draw your own pictures to show 2 × 3 and 2 × 10.

I am confident with using multiplication arrays.

Find out which numbers of plants can be grown in rectangles with more than one row.

My plants all grow in rectangles. Each rectangle must have more than one row!

		Can be	Cannot be
3 plants			✔
4 plants		✔	

Try all the numbers from I to 20. Draw a table and fill it in.

Number of plants	Can be	Cannot be
I		✔
2		✔
3		✔
4	✔	

THINK Which numbers can be grown in more than one rectangle?

Multiplying by 2, 3 and 5

Work out how many coins are needed to make the amounts.

How many 2p coins will I need to make 6p?

 $3 \times 2p = 6p$

1 ☐ $\times 2p = 8p$

2 ☐ $\times 2p = 4p$

3 ☐ $\times 2p = 12p$

4 ☐ $\times 5p = 10p$

5 ☐ $\times 5p = 25p$

6 ☐ $\times 5p = 15p$

How many 3-leafed clovers are needed to make the amounts of leaves?

7 ☐ $\times 3 = 6$ leaves

8 ☐ $\times 3 = 9$ leaves

9 ☐ $\times 3 = 15$ leaves

10 ☐ $\times 3 = 30$ leaves

11 ☐ $\times 3 = 21$ leaves

THINK How many clovers do you need for 30 leaves?
How many do you need for 300 leaves?

○
○ **I am confident with multiplying by 2, 3 and 5.**
○

Multiplying by 3 and 4

**Copy and complete the number line.
Carry on the jumps to 30.**

| 0 | 3 | 6 | 9 | 12 | 15 |

1 $4 \times 3 = \square$ **3** $\square \times 3 = 24$ **5** $\square \times 3 = 9$

2 $6 \times 3 = \square$ **4** $\square \times 3 = 21$ **6** $9 \times 3 = \square$

**Copy and complete the number line.
Carry on the jumps to 40.**

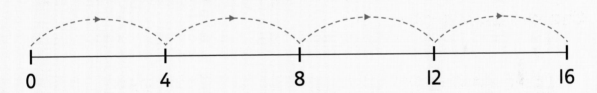

| 0 | 4 | 8 | 12 | 16 |

7 $\square \times 4 = 20$ **9** $9 \times 4 = \square$ **11** $\square \times 4 = 16$

8 $8 \times 4 = \square$ **10** $\square \times 4 = 28$ **12** $6 \times 4 = \square$

THINK Look at the first six multiplications.
Not all of the 3s count is here. Can
you write the missing multiplications?

I am confident with multiplying by 3 and 4.

Measuring length

Use a ruler to measure the length of each insect.

Draw three more insects and measure their lengths to the nearest centimetre.

○ I am confident with measuring length in cm.
○
○

Measure the lines with a ruler and write the lengths in centimetres.

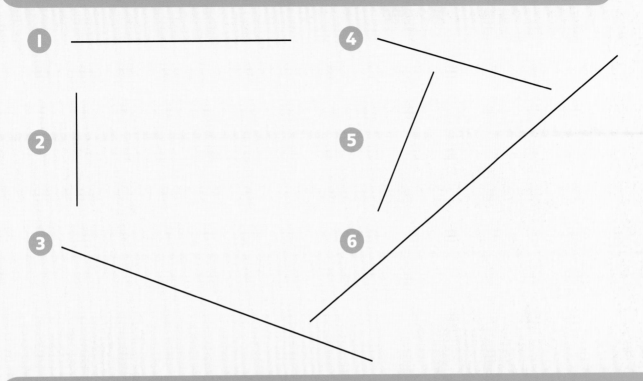

① _____

② (vertical line)

③ (angled line)

④ (angled line)

⑤ (angled line)

⑥ (angled line)

Estimate the length of each object. Write down which measurement you think is more likely to be correct.

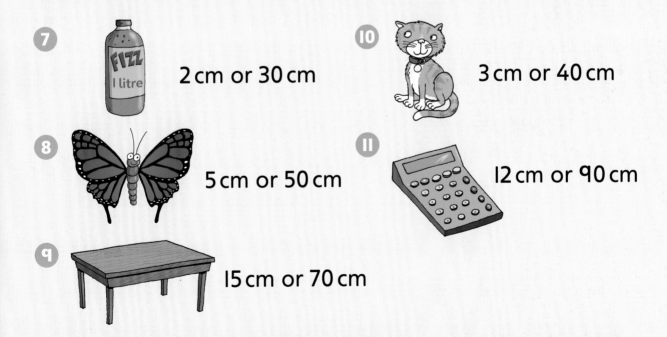

⑦ 2 cm or 30 cm

⑧ 5 cm or 50 cm

⑨ 15 cm or 70 cm

⑩ 3 cm or 40 cm

⑪ 12 cm or 90 cm

I am confident with measuring and estimating in cm.

Reading temperatures

Write the cooler temperature first, then write the hotter temperature. Write a temperature that comes between them.

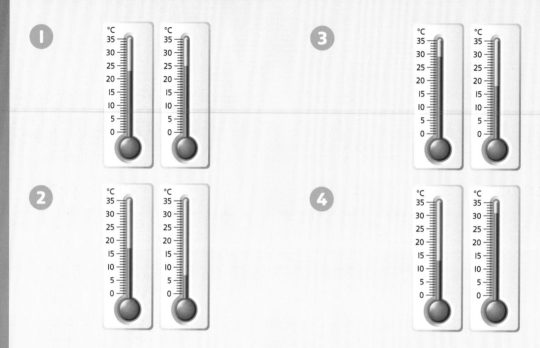

Order the temperatures from coolest to hottest.

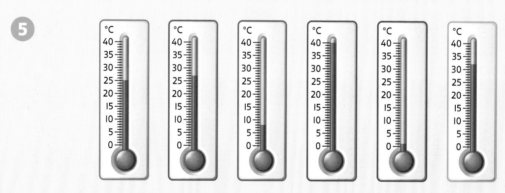

 THINK What is the hottest temperature and the coolest temperature on this page? Find a temperature on this page that is in-between.

○
○ I am confident with reading and comparing
○ temperatures.

Write the temperatures in order from coolest to hottest.

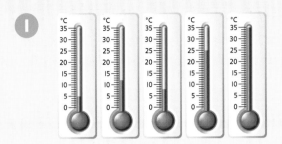

Work out the difference between the day temperature and the night temperature.

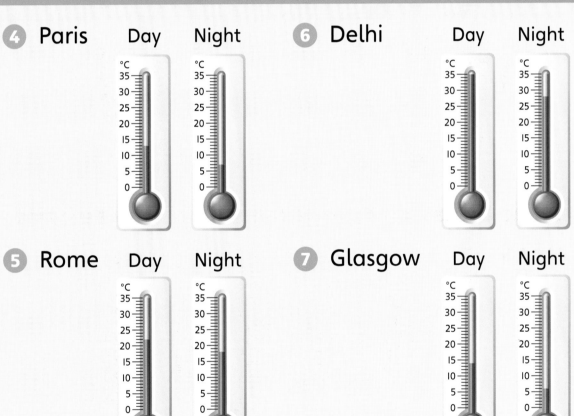

4 Paris Day Night

6 Delhi Day Night

5 Rome Day Night

7 Glasgow Day Night

THINK

What could the day and night temperatures in London be if the difference between them is 5 degrees?

Hundreds, tens and ones

GRAB! Place-value cards

Write the addition sentences in full, including the missing numbers.

👉 100 + 30 + 4 = 1 3 4

1. 100 + 30 + ☐ = 1 3 4

2. 200 + 60 + 4 = ☐☐☐

3. 400 + ☐ + 7 = 4 8 7

4. ☐ + 70 + 5 = 2 7 5

5. 500 + ☐ + 4 = 5 8 4

6. 30 + 400 + 7 = ☐☐☐

7. ☐ + ☐ + 600 = 6 4 2

8. ☐ + 400 + 7 = 4 2 7

9. ☐ + 1 + 300 = 3 7 1

10. ☐ + 1 + ☐ = 5 6 1

THINK How many 3-digit numbers that are less than 500 have a 0 in their 10s place?

○
○ **I am confident with reading and writing hundreds,**
○ **tens and ones.**

Practising calculations

1. 24 + 71 = □

2. 3 + 8 + 7 = □

3. 5 + 9 + 5 = □

4. 34 + 25 = □

5. 84 − 52 = □

6. 68 − 45 = □

7. 4 × 3 = □

8. 6 × 3 = □

9. 43 + □ = 68

10. 7 + 7 + 5 = □

11. 8 + 4 + 6 = □

12. □ × 3 = 9

13. 86 − 45 = □

14. 84 − 71 = □

15. □ × 3 = 27

16. □ × 3 = 21

17. Rani has four coins. Two are 5p coins and two are 2p coin. How much money does she have?

18. On Ellie's birthday she brings in sweets for her class. The bag holds 48 sweets. All 27 children in the class get one sweet. How many sweets are left in the pack?

19. There are 59 hippos. 36 are cooling off in the water. How many are not in the water?

20. A pet shop has 3 guinea-pigs, 7 hamsters and 8 gerbils. How many animals are there in total?

Series Editor
Ruth Merttens

Author Team
Jennie Kerwin and Hilda Merttens

Published by Pearson Education Limited, Edinburgh Gate, Harlow, Essex, CM20 2JE.

www.pearsonschools.co.uk

Additional contributions by Hilary Koll and Steve Mills, CME Projects Ltd.

First published 2014

16
10 9 8 7 6 5

British Library Cataloguing in Publication Data
A catalogue record for this book is available from the British Library

ISBN 978 1 408 27824 6

Acknowledgements
We would like to thank the staff and pupils at North Kidlington Primary School, Haydon Wick Primary School, Swindon, St Mary's Catholic Primary School, Bodmin, St Andrew's C of E Primary & Nursery School, Sutton-in-Ashfield, Saint James' C of E Primary School, Southampton and Harborne Primary School, Birmingham, for their invaluable help in the development and trialling of this book.

Every effort has been made to contact copyright holders of material reproduced in this book. Any omissions will be rectified in subsequent printings if notice is given to the publishers.